ECOFACTS

NATURAL RESOURCES

ECO FACTS

IZZI HOWELL

CRABTREE
PUBLISHING COMPANY
WWW.CRABTREEBOOKS.COM

CRABTREE
PUBLISHING COMPANY
WWW.CRABTREEBOOKS.COM

Author: Izzi Howell

Editorial director: Kathy Middleton

Editors: Izzi Howell, Ellen Rodger

Proofreader: Melissa Boyce

Designer: Clare Nicholas

Cover designer: Steve Mead

Prepress technician: Tammy McGarr

Print coordinator: Katherine Berti

Photo credits:
Alamy: Planetpix 11b; Getty: Stockbyte 11t, Kiyoshi Ota/Bloomberg 19, ALBERT GONZALEZ FARRAN/AFP 23, simonkr 26; Shutterstock: hxdbzxy 5, Roel Slootweg 7, Wisit Tongma 8, Kletr 12, Dr Morley Read 15, salajean 17, DJTaylor 21, MicheleB 22, Marcio Jose Bastos Silva 24, Rido 29.

All design elements from Shutterstock.

Every attempt has been made to clear copyright. Should there be any inadvertent omission please apply to the publisher for rectification.

The website addresses (URLs) included in this book were valid at the time of going to press. However, it is possible that contents or addresses may have changed since the publication of this book. No responsibility for any such changes can be accepted by either the author or the Publisher.

Library and Archives Canada Cataloguing in Publication

Title: Natural resources eco facts / Izzi Howell.
Names: Howell, Izzi, author.
Description: Series statement: Eco facts | Includes index.
Identifiers: Canadiana (print) 20190087978 |
  Canadiana (ebook) 20190087986 |
  ISBN 9780778763475 (hardcover) |
  ISBN 9780778763635 (softcover) |
  ISBN 9781427123459 (HTML)
Subjects: LCSH: Natural resources—Environmental aspects—
  Juvenile literature. | LCSH: Nature—Effect of human beings on—
  Juvenile literature.
Classification: LCC HC85 .H69 2019 | DDC j333.7—dc23

Library of Congress Cataloging-in-Publication Data

Names: Howell, Izzi, author.
Title: Natural resources eco facts / Izzi Howell.
Description: New York : Crabtree Publishing Company, 2019. |
Series: Eco facts | Includes index. |
Identifiers: LCCN 2019014215 (print) | LCCN 2019019538 (ebook) |
  ISBN 9781427123459 (Electronic) |
  ISBN 9780778763475 (hardcover) |
  ISBN 9780778763635 (pbk.)
Subjects: LCSH: Natural resources--Juvenile literature. |
  Conservation of natural resources--Juvenile literature.
Classification: LCC HC85 (ebook) | LCC HC85 .H683 2019 (print) |
  DDC 333.7--dc23
LC record available at https://lccn.loc.gov/2019014215

Crabtree Publishing Company

www.crabtreebooks.com   1–800–387–7650

Published by Crabtree Publishing Company in 2020
©2019 The Watts Publishing Group.

Printed in the U.S.A./072019/CG20190501

Published in Canada
Crabtree Publishing
616 Welland Ave.
St. Catharines, Ontario
L2M 5V6

Published in the United States
Crabtree Publishing
PMB 59051
350 Fifth Avenue, 59th Floor
New York, New York 10118

Contents

What are natural resources?............ 4

Resource distribution 6

Oil, gas, and coal........................... 8

(FOCUS ON) Arctic oil 10

Wood 12

(FOCUS ON) Reforestation 14

Metal and stone 16

(FOCUS ON) Rare earth metals 18

Water 20

Farming 22

Wildlife 24

(FOCUS ON) Bees 25

Recycling.. 26

Managing natural resources 28

Glossary 30

Learning More................................. 31

Index 32

What are natural resources?

Natural resources are things we use that come from nature, such as wood, metal, and water. We use these resources for construction, food, and technology, as well as to produce energy and power vehicles.

Renewable resources

Natural resources can be **renewable** or **nonrenewable**. The supply of renewable resources will never run out. The amount of these resources, which include sunlight, water, and wind, always stays the same. Some natural resources, such as plants and **crops** for food, can be regrown. As long as we continue to plant these resources, our supply will not run out.

Natural resources on Earth include...

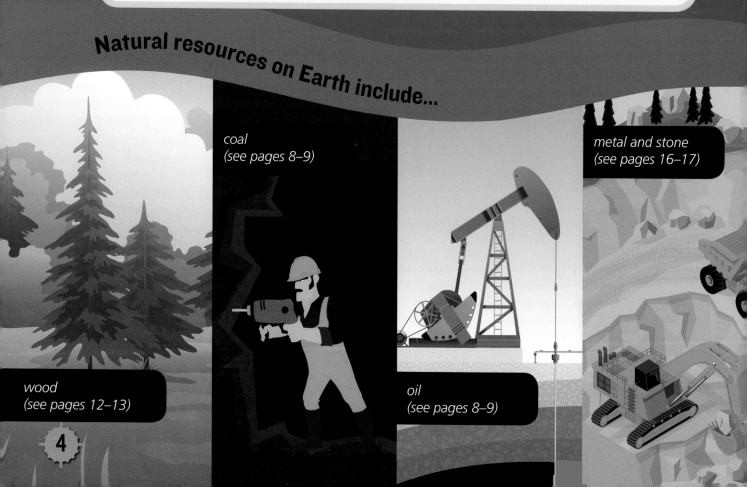

coal
(see pages 8–9)

metal and stone
(see pages 16–17)

wood
(see pages 12–13)

oil
(see pages 8–9)

Nonrenewable resources

Other natural resources are nonrenewable, such as natural gas, oil, coal, and certain minerals. We have a limited amount of these resources, as it takes millions of years for them to form. At the moment, we are not using these resources in a **sustainable** way. If we continue to use them at current rates, our supply will eventually run out.

We use a huge amount of gasoline, made from oil, as fuel for vehicles such as cars, planes, and trucks.

Consequences

Using some resources has a negative impact on the environment. Burning **fossil fuels**, such as coal, oil, and natural gas, causes the temperature on Earth to rise (see page 9). Cutting down trees for timber and clearing forests for farmland destroys **ecosystems** and affects plant and animal life.

crops
(see pages 22–23)

bees
(see page 25)

water
(see pages 20–21)

fish
(see page 24)

Resource distribution

Some areas around the world have more natural resources than others. The amount of resources used by people is different in every country.

Raw materials

Many resources come from poorer countries. They supply **raw** materials such as metals, timber, and some crops. Some of these resources are made into goods such as cars, mobile phones, or furniture.

Trade

Trade allows countries to get resources that they need that are not available in their country. However, trade depends on the wealth of the country. Not every country can buy all the resources that its citizens need.

Using resources

The amount of resources used in different countries varies a lot. People in wealthier countries consume far more resources than people in less wealthy countries. They own more objects, drive larger cars, and live in bigger houses that require more energy to run.

Average quantity of resources used every day per person in North America and Africa:

198 pounds (90 kg) North America

22 pounds (10 kg) Africa

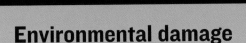

Environmental damage

Less economically developed countries can grow economically and become more developed by selling their resources. However, **extracting** these resources can have a serious impact on the environment in these countries. Drilling for oil and using **pesticides** in farming and mining can damage the land and kill animals and plants. Deforestation can in turn lead to **desertification**, where the land turns into a desert.

This lake in Madagascar has been polluted and turned red by waste from a mine.

Population size

The use of resources is linked to population size. As the global population increases, so will the **demand** for resources. There are already 7.6 billion people on Earth, but this number may rise to over 9 billion by 2050. Earth may not contain enough resources to support such a high population, especially if people use excessive quantities of resources—for example, by living in very large houses that require a lot of energy to run.

We currently extract
66 billion tons
(60 billion metric tons)
of resources every year.
By 2030, we may
need to extract
110 billion tons
(100 billion metric tons)
to support the
world population.

Oil, gas, and coal

Oil, natural gas, and coal are valuable resources that are burned as fuel and used to generate electricity. They are nonrenewable resources, and there is a real risk that they may run out within the next 100 years.

Fossil fuels

Oil, natural gas, and coal are known as fossil fuels. They formed over millions of years from the remains of dead plants and animals. They are found underground.

Drilling for oil and natural gas

To access oil and natural gas, workers drill holes deep in the ground. They use pumps to draw the resources up to the surface. **Reserves** of oil and natural gas are often found in the rock underneath the seabed.

Oil platforms are structures built on bodies of water, with equipment to drill and store oil and natural gas. Ships carry the oil and natural gas to shore.

Coal mines

Most coal is dug out of mines deep underground. In some areas, the entire top of a mountain is removed to access the coal inside.

Creating electricity

Fossil fuels are burned in power plants to generate electricity. When they are burned, they create heat, which is used to boil water. The boiling water makes steam, which makes a turbine spin. The spinning turbine powers a generator, which produces electricity.

The end of fossil fuels

Our supply of fossil fuels is running low. We have the smallest current reserves of oil, followed by natural gas and coal.

2052 **Oil—We are currently using 12.1 billion tons (11 billion metric tons) a year. If this continues, we will run out by around 2052.**

2060 **Natural gas—Use of natural gas will probably increase after our oil supplies run out. Due to this increase, supplies of natural gas will run out around 2060.**

2088 **Coal—After natural gas and oil run out, use of coal will probably increase as well. Because of this, supplies will probably only last until around 2088.**

Fracking

Fracking is a method of extracting natural gas and oil that are trapped inside shale rock. Water, sand, and chemicals are injected into the rock to break it apart so that the natural gas and oil are released. As supplies of fossil fuels run low, fracking is one way of accessing more resources. However, the process is **controversial**. It damages the environment through its heavy use of water and poisonous chemicals, and it may even cause small earthquakes.

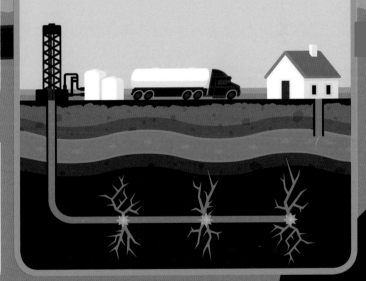

The greenhouse effect

When fossil fuels are burned, they release carbon dioxide. This gas gathers in the **atmosphere** around Earth. It traps heat energy from the Sun's light, which increases the temperature on Earth and leads to **climate change**. This is known as the greenhouse effect.

9

Arctic oil

As oil begins to run out in some areas, oil companies are starting to look for new places to drill. The Arctic seabed is one site where oil and natural gas could be extracted, but at great risk to the environment.

Up to **160** billion barrels of oil could lie under the Arctic seabed.

Why now?

In the past, oil companies didn't have the technology to extract oil from under the deep Arctic seabed. New equipment and technology will make this process simpler and safer. Blocks of sheet ice that previously covered the Arctic Ocean are now melting because of climate change. This makes it easier for ships to reach these areas.

More oil

Some people are concerned about drilling for oil in the Arctic because they don't think that we should be extracting more oil to be used as fuel. Burning this oil will contribute to further climate change. Many scientists think it's better to leave any remaining oil in the ground and instead invest in alternative sources of energy that are less damaging to the environment (see page 28).

Threats

Drilling for oil in the Arctic will also damage fragile ecosystems. Chemicals used in drilling will poison the water, affecting fish and other animals that depend on fish for food. Loud drilling noises will travel through the water, disturbing animals that use sound to navigate, such as dolphins and whales.

There is a
75 percent
chance of a
major oil spill
if Arctic oil
is extracted.

An environmental charity organizes a protest against Arctic oil drilling in Washington, D.C. Charities are trying to create new protected areas in the Arctic to help save the animals that live there.

Fighting back

Environmental charities are trying to stop drilling for Arctic oil by taking countries to court. They believe that plans to drill for more oil mean that the countries are breaking climate-change agreements. In the meantime, scientists are trying to develop new oil-drilling methods and transport systems that are less likely to spill and damage the Arctic environment.

Wood

Wood is a renewable resource. If our supply of wood is managed properly, it will not run out. In some areas, however, wood is being gathered in an unsustainable way. Chopping down trees is also damaging some ecosystems.

Uses

Wood is used in many ways. It is a building material for houses, furniture, and other structures. It can also be processed to make paper and cardboard. In some countries, wood is burned as a fuel, either in wood stoves for heat, or to cook food where people do not have electric or gas stoves.

Logging

The process of cutting down trees is called logging. Loggers use huge, powerful saws to cut through the trunk of a tree. The trunks are then sent to sawmills, where they are cut into smaller pieces of wood. Most countries have rules about the quantity and type of trees loggers can cut down. This protects woodland and forest ecosystems.

Illegal logging

In some countries, such as Russia, Brazil, and Indonesia, loggers work illegally. They cut down too many trees, or gather wood from protected areas or endangered trees. This reduces biodiversity in woodlands and forests, as these trees provide food and shelter for animals and plants. It also takes money away from local communities that depend on legal logging for their income.

Loggers use mechanical arms to pick up the heavy logs. They transport them to the sawmill by truck.

Sustainable logging

Sustainable logging is one way of producing timber while still protecting the environment. Instead of cutting down wild trees, farmers plant huge amounts of the same type of fast-growing tree on a tree plantation. These trees are cut down when they are ready, and more trees are planted in their place. This secures the supply of wood for the future.

Deforestation

Not all trees are cut down to be used for their wood. In some regions, such as Southeast Asia and Brazil, large areas of rain forest are cut down so that the land can be used for farming or construction. This is known as **deforestation**.

Half of the world's rain forests have been cut down or cleared in the last 100 years.

One small step

Buy notepads, books, and greeting cards with the FSC logo. This shows that the wood used to make the paper comes from sustainable forests.

Forest fires

Forest fires are a natural threat to our wood supply. They are sometimes started when lightning hits dry plants, and sets them on fire. The fire then spreads rapidly through the nearby area, destroying any trees and plants in its path. Forest fires are becoming more common because of **global warming**. Human activity can also start forest fires.

Reforestation

Rain forests and woodlands can be brought back to life by planting new trees. This is called reforestation. However, it has to be done carefully or the ecosystem will not recover properly.

Around the world

Many countries are starting to realize the importance of forests. They are planning large-scale reforestation to recover the trees that have been destroyed through logging or land clearance.

Tree plantations

Not all reforestation is good for biodiversity. Planting with just one type of fast-growing tree is a sustainable way of producing wood and protecting wild forests (see page 13). However, these trees may not provide the right food or shelter for animals that previously lived in the habitat.

Recovering biodiversity

To create new, biodiverse forest habitats, different species of trees need to be planted. Each species provides food and shelter for different animals. It's also important to plant **native** trees. Introduced trees may disturb the balance of the ecosystem and affect the growth of native trees by blocking their light or absorbing too much water from the ground.

Some animals live high in the branches of tall trees, while others live in low trees, closer to the ground.

Difficulties

Reforestation needs to be carefully managed. Newly planted trees require a great deal of water while they are growing. Some trees may need to be watered, as there isn't enough rain to keep them alive. Looking after new trees is expensive. Many poorer countries, which suffer the most from deforestation to begin with, cannot afford the costs.

Agroforestry

In agroforestry, crops are planted around wild forests, allowing both plants and trees to grow together. This is a good solution to deforestation for less economically developed countries. The trees' leaves provide shade for the crops and protect them from heavy rain.

In this agroforestry farm in Ecuador, coffee plants are grown among native rainforest trees.

15

Metal and stone

Metal and stone are dug out of the ground. They are used for construction, technology, and to make jewellery.

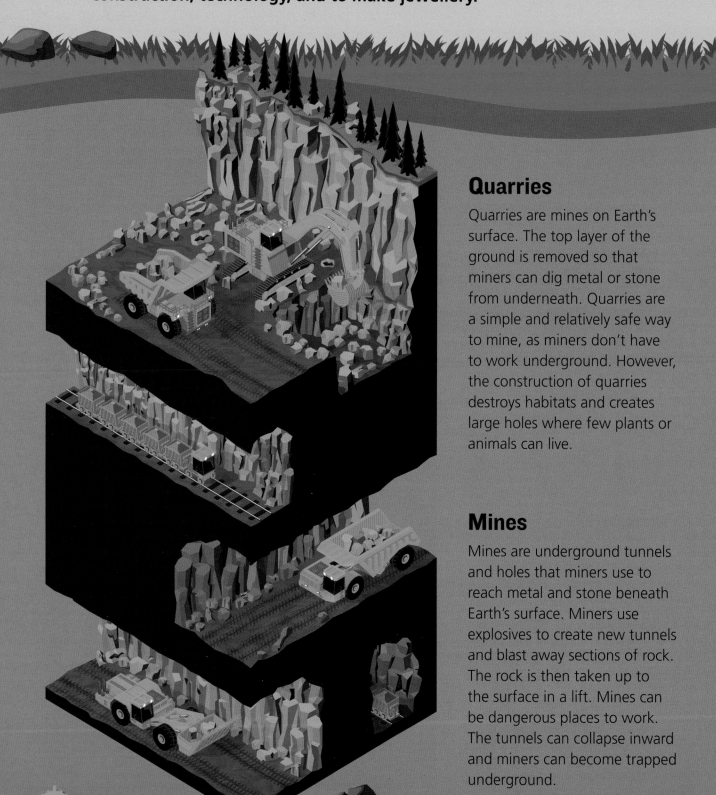

Quarries

Quarries are mines on Earth's surface. The top layer of the ground is removed so that miners can dig metal or stone from underneath. Quarries are a simple and relatively safe way to mine, as miners don't have to work underground. However, the construction of quarries destroys habitats and creates large holes where few plants or animals can live.

Mines

Mines are underground tunnels and holes that miners use to reach metal and stone beneath Earth's surface. Miners use explosives to create new tunnels and blast away sections of rock. The rock is then taken up to the surface in a lift. Mines can be dangerous places to work. The tunnels can collapse inward and miners can become trapped underground.

Rock to metal

Most metals do not exist in a pure state in the ground. They are found as an **ore**—a mixture of metal and other minerals. For example, aluminum is nearly always found as bauxite ore, rather than as pure aluminum. Metal ore is heated until the metal melts and can be separated from the other minerals.

Supply

Metal and stone are nonrenewable resources. However, there is still a large amount of these resources left in the ground, so we are not at risk of running out soon.

Environmental impact

Mining metal and stone has a negative impact on the environment. Chemicals used in mining are washed onto nearby land, polluting it and harming the plants and animals that live there. The machines used to drill into the ground and transport metal and stone also run on fossil fuels, which contribute to the greenhouse effect.

The water in this lake in Romania has turned red because of iron pollution from mining.

Reuse and recycle

To avoid further environmental damage caused by mining, it is much better for us to reuse and recycle the stone and metal that we have already gathered, rather than collecting more. This will also help us to preserve our supply of these resources for the future.

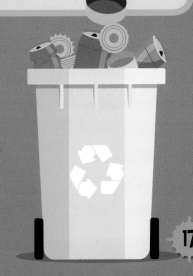

Rare earth metals

Rare earth metals are a group of 17 metals that are used in almost every kind of modern technology, from headphones to wind turbines. These metals are plentiful in Earth's crust but rare to find in one spot. Some rare earth metals and their products include...

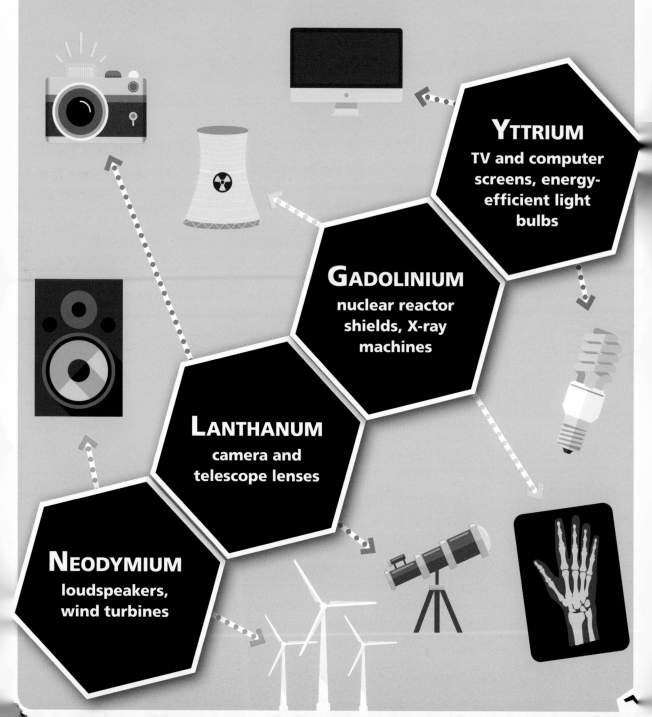

YTTRIUM
TV and computer screens, energy-efficient light bulbs

GADOLINIUM
nuclear reactor shields, X-ray machines

LANTHANUM
camera and telescope lenses

NEODYMIUM
loudspeakers, wind turbines

Sources

There are large amounts of rare earth metals in Earth's crust. However, these metals are spread out over a huge area and it is unusual to find many in one place. They are nearly always found mixed with other minerals in ores. For this reason, sourcing rare earth metals is a slow and difficult process.

Location

Around 90 percent of the world's supply of rare earth metals comes from mines in China. This is a potential problem, as it means that China could stop other countries from making technology by cutting off their supply of rare earth metals or by raising the prices too high. Other areas are currently being surveyed for rare earth minerals, including Japan, the U.S., and Brazil.

Scientists believe that they have found a source of **15.9 million tons** (14.5 million metric tons) of rare earth metals in the seabed off the coast of Japan.

Demand and supply

At the moment, the demand for rare earth metals is greater than its supply. This is due to the explosion in new technology that has taken place over the past 20 years. As new types of technology are developed and demand continues to grow, we may face a shortage of rare earth metals in the future.

Recycling

Some of the rare earth metals in pieces of technology can be recycled. This helps to reduce the demand for mined metals and stops these metals from being wasted in landfills. However, only small amounts of rare earth metals are used in devices such as mobile phones, so it is very difficult to extract them and recycle them.

A worker at a rare earth metal recycling facility in Japan sorts through old devices for recycling.

Water

Water is a very important resource. It isn't just used for drinking. It's also needed for industry, agriculture, and household use, such as washing machines.

Only **2.5 percent** of water on Earth is freshwater.

Water on Earth

Almost all of the water on Earth is saltwater, found in the oceans. There is only a very small amount of the freshwater that humans need for most tasks. This makes it a rare and valuable resource.

Using water

Wealthier countries use much more water than poorer countries. This is because people in wealthier countries tend to waste more in their daily use by letting taps run, taking long showers and baths.

Finding water

Freshwater is found in lakes and rivers. It can also be pumped up from below the ground. In some dry areas with few lakes or rivers, salt is removed from seawater so that the water can be used for drinking and cleaning. However, this process is very expensive and consumes a lot of electricity.

Industry and agriculture

Most of the water consumed in poorer countries is used in industry and agriculture. Water is used in fossil fuel power stations to generate electricity (see page 8), which is used to power factories. Raising animals to eat for food also uses water, which is needed for the animals to drink and for growing food for them to eat.

The
amount of
water needed
to produce
2.2 pounds
(1 kg) of food:

beef— 4,072 gallons (15,415 L)
chicken—1,142 gallons (4,325 L)
rice—660 gallons (2,497 L)
bread—425 gallons (1,608 L)
apples—218 gallons (822 L)
potatoes—76 gallons (287 L)

Clean water

Water in lakes and rivers can contain bacteria that can make people sick. These bacteria can come from human waste or pollution. Water is treated to kill the bacteria before it travels through pipes into people's homes.

Around the world

Many people do not have a reliable water supply. They have no water pipes in their homes or villages. They have to walk long distances to gather water from wells and carry it back to their homes. Sometimes, they have no choice other than to use untreated water from lakes and rivers.

Using less water

Freshwater is a valuable resource that we must not waste. Factories can recycle the water that they use, rather than using new water. At home, people could use water from baths or showers to water their plants.

This woman has collected water in a rain barrel, which she is using to water her plants.

One small step

Turn off the tap while brushing your teeth. A running tap uses 1.6 gallons (6 L) of water per minute.

Farming

Farmers grow crops and raise animals to provide people with food. Some people worry that climate change and the world's growing population may make it harder for us to produce enough food in the future.

Crops

Fruits, vegetables, and grains are crops grown by farmers. They need water and fertile soil to grow. They are very important to our food supply. Grains, such as rice and wheat, provide the main part of most people's diets around the world.

A farmer in China harvests a field of rice.

Rice provides over **one-fifth** of all calories eaten around the world.

Problems

There are many issues that threaten our food supply. Very high temperatures and **drought**, caused by global warming, can kill crops before they are ready to eat. Cleared forest land is often not very fertile. It can be hard for farmers to grow crops on it. Crops are also at risk because of the decline of bee populations (see page 25).

Import and export

Many crops are grown in poorer countries. They are often exported to wealthier countries to be eaten. Transporting food around the world creates pollution and **greenhouse gases**.

One small step

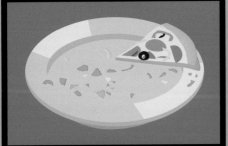

Try to use up every bit of food that you buy. Save leftover food from dinner for lunch the next day.

Hunger and famine

Many people around the world do not have a secure food supply. This isn't because there is not enough food to go around, but because of poverty. People in less economically developed countries may not earn enough money to buy food, so they go hungry. When crops fail, countries often do not have enough money to import food for their citizens. This can lead to **famine** and death.

Women in South Sudan measure out donated corn in 2017. South Sudan has been seriously affected by drought and famine, despite food aid from other countries.

GM crops

Scientists have created **genetically modified (GM)** crops that are more **resistant** to high temperatures and poor growing conditions. They also produce more food. Some people believe that GM crops will help us to protect our food supply. Others worry that there may be long-term problems with eating GM crops, as there hasn't been much research done yet.

Wildlife

Wild plants and animals are an important resource. Some species, such as fish, are a source of food. Others carry out important roles that help us to survive.

Fish

Fish are one of the few wild animals that we eat in large numbers. We also eat some fish that are raised on farms. Our supply of fish has been affected by fishers catching too many of them, especially young fish. They don't leave enough fish to reproduce, so the population can't recover. Rules that control the size and number of fish that fishers can catch have helped fish populations to grow again.

The number of cod in the North Sea has multiplied by 4 since 2006!

Plants

Photosynthesis is the process by which plants produce energy. Plants release oxygen during photosynthesis. Humans breathe in oxygen. Without plants on Earth, there would not be enough oxygen for humans to survive.

Pollination

Animals such as bees and butterflies help to **pollinate** wild plants. When they land on flowers to drink nectar, pollen sticks to their legs. They carry this pollen to every flower that they visit, fertilizing the other flowers. Without pollination, plants would not produce seeds for new plants. We would lose our supply of strawberries, cotton, and potatoes, among others.

Around 70 percent of the oxygen in the atmosphere is produced by marine plants, such as kelp and plankton.

carbon dioxide

oxygen

FOCUS ON Bees

Bees play an important role in the pollination of plants. However, some species of bees are dying out. Our food supply will be seriously affected if bees continue to disappear.

Why?

Different species of bees are declining for different reasons.

Pesticides

Some pesticides that are used to kill crop-destroying insects also harm bees. They damage the bees' ability to navigate, reproduce, and fly.

Habitat loss

The wildflower meadows where some bees feed on nectar and pollen are being destroyed and turned into farmland.

Climate change

Flowers are blooming earlier in the year because of global warming. Some bees don't come out of their hive until later, when the flowers used to bloom. They miss the opportunity for food and so they starve.

Diseases

Recent outbreaks of bee diseases have affected some species around the world.

One small step

Grow flowering plants that bees like to visit, such as lavender, sunflowers, and apple trees, in the school playground or at home.

Solutions

There are several ways we can help to protect bees. The European Union has already banned some pesticides that harm bees. Protecting and replanting wildflower areas will create new sources of food for hungry bees.

Recycling

Recycling is a great way of using fewer resources. It also cuts down on pollution and energy use.

Things to recycle

Many items can be recycled. In most areas, paper, cardboard, plastic, glass, metal, and textiles can be recycled. In many places, recycling is collected from people's houses.

Recycling materials uses 95 percent less energy than making new materials from scratch.

Workers at a recycling plant sort paper on a conveyor belt.

One small step

Try a paper recycling challenge at home or at school for one week. Every unwanted piece of paper must be recycled—nothing can go in the trash!

Recycling problems

Recycling does consume some resources. Plastic is used to make recycling containers and bins. Fuel is needed to power recycling collection vehicles and the machines at recycling plants.

Reduce and reuse

Reusing objects and reducing the amount you consume is even better for the environment than recycling. This is because no new resources or energy are needed, unlike recycling. If everyone reduced or reused a few objects, it would make a big difference. Try using reusable water bottles and shopping bags, and buying clothes and other items from secondhand or thrift stores instead of new.

Landfill

If objects aren't reused or recycled, they are often sent to landfill sites when they are thrown away. Landfill sites are dumps where garbage is stored. Glass, plastic, and metal can take millions of years to break down, so these objects will stay in the soil for a long time. Landfill sites pollute the ground around them, so the land can't be reused unless it is rehabilitated, or cleaned up. They also create greenhouse gases, such as methane, which contribute to global warming.

Burning waste

In some places, garbage is burned in incinerators. This reduces the amount of waste sent to landfill sites. However, burning waste releases greenhouse gases and toxic gases that can cause breathing problems and other health issues for people who live nearby.

Food waste

We can't recycle food, but we can make compost from food waste, such as leftover bread and meat, fruit and vegetable peelings, and eggshells. In the right conditions, this waste quickly breaks down and becomes compost. Compost can be added to soil to fertilize it so that crops can grow better.

Managing natural resources

It's important to manage the remaining natural resources on Earth. This will save them for future generations to use and help to preserve the environment.

Renewable energy

More and more countries are working on changing from nonrenewable to renewable sources of energy, such as solar, wind, and hydroelectric power, and **geothermal** energy, or heat from Earth. Renewable energy reduces the use of fossil fuels and prevents further climate change.

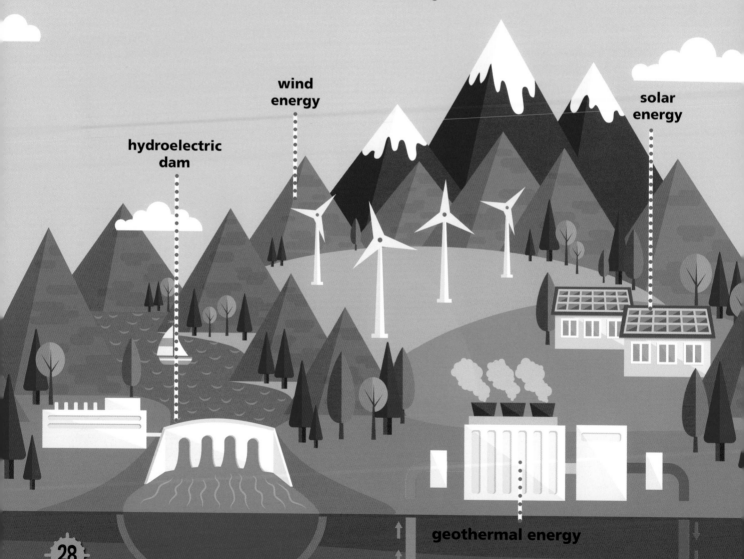

wind
energy

hydroelectric
dam

solar
energy

geothermal energy

The age of electricity

Some car manufacturers are now producing cars that run partly or entirely on electricity, rather than gas made from oil. Driving an electric car uses fewer resources. If the electricity used to power the car comes from renewable sources, electric cars are a very sustainable form of transportation. Vehicles that run on biofuel, or fuel that comes from plants, are also becoming increasingly popular.

Organic fruits and vegetables are grown without pesticides that harm insects. By eating organic food where possible, we can help protect insects such as bees.

A recovering world

It's not too late to undo the damage done to the planet through the overuse of resources. We can replant trees sustainably (see page 15), and help plant and animal life to return. By following rules about sustainable fishing and pesticide use, fish and insect populations should eventually be restored.

Doing our part

Industries and governments have the most responsibility for managing resources wisely. However, we can all help. Try to use less water at home and at school. Reduce, reuse, and recycle as much as you can. See if your school can install solar panels to produce some of the electricity it uses.

One small step

Talk to your friends and family about using natural resources responsibly. Share some of the ideas in this book with them.

Glossary

atmosphere The layer of gases around Earth

climate change Changes to the weather on Earth

controversial A topic that is argued over

crops Plants that are grown in large amounts

deforestation Cutting down trees and clearing land

demand A need for something to be supplied or sold

desertification When fertile land turns into a desert

drought A period when there isn't enough water

ecosystem All the living things in an area

extract To take something out

famine A long period of time when people in an area do not have enough food

fossil fuel A fuel that comes from the ground, such as coal, oil, or natural gas

genetically modify (GM) To alter characteristics of a crop to help it grow better

geothermal The heat inside Earth

global warming An increase in the temperature around the world because of the greenhouse effect

greenhouse gas A gas that traps heat in the atmosphere, such as carbon dioxide

native Something that grows or lives naturally in a place and has not been brought from somewhere else

nonrenewable Describes something that can't be reproduced and can run out

ore A mixture of metal and other minerals

pesticide A chemical used to kill insects and other living things that harm plants

pollinate To transfer pollen from one plant to another, producing seeds

raw A resource that has not been processed

renewable Describes something that can be reproduced and will not run out

reserve The amount of something that is left

resistant Not harmed or affected by something

sustainable Describes something that can continue for a long time because it does not harm the environment

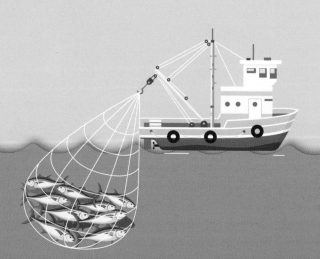

Learning More

Books

Dickmann, Nancy. **Leaving Our Mark: Reducing Our Carbon Footprint.** Crabtree Publishing, 2016.

Howell, Izzi. **Earth's Resources Geo Facts.** Crabtree Publishing, 2018.

Washburne, Sophie. **Alternative Energy Sources: The End of Fossil Fuels?** Lucent Books, 2019.

Websites

climatekids.nasa.gov/recycle-this/
Play a recycling game and learn recycling facts.

www.theworldcounts.com
See in real time how resources are used.

www.bbc.co.uk/guides/ztxwqty
Find out more about renewable and nonrenewable sources of energy.

www.epa.gov/watersense/watersense-kids
Learn simple ways to save water.

Index

Arctic, the 10, 11

bees 5, 22, 24, 25, 29

climate change 10, 11, 22, 25, 28
coal 4, 5, 8–9
crops 4, 5, 6, 15, 22–23, 25, 27

deforestation 7, 13, 15
desertification 7

electricity 8, 12, 20, 29

farming 5, 7, 13, 15, 22–23, 25
fish 5, 11, 24, 29
forest fires 13
fossil fuels 5, 8, 17, 20
fracking 9

global warming 13, 25, 27, 28
greenhouse effect 9, 17
greenhouse gases 23, 27

landfill 19, 27

metal 4, 6, 16–17, 18, 19, 26, 27
minerals 5, 17, 19
mines 7, 8, 16, 17, 19

natural gas 5, 8–9, 10
nonrenewable resources 4, 5, 8, 17, 28

oil 4, 5, 7, 8–9, 10, 11, 29
oil spills 11
ore 17

photosynthesis 24
pollination 24, 25
pollution 7, 9, 11, 17, 21, 23, 27
population 7

quarries 16

rare earth metals 18–19
raw materials 6
recycling 17, 19, 21, 26–27, 29
reforestation 14–15, 29
renewable resources 4, 12, 28, 29

stone 4, 16–17

trade 6

water 4, 5, 15, 20–21, 22, 29
wood 4, 12–13, 14, 15